IT'S YOUR CHOICE!

IT'S YOUR CHOICE!

BY TERRENCE FOX

TATE PUBLISHING
AND ENTERPRISES, LLC

Published by Tate Publishing & Enterprises, LLC
127 E. Trade Center Terrace | Mustang, Oklahoma 73064 USA
1.888.361.9473 | www.tatepublishing.com

Tate Publishing is committed to excellence in the publishing industry. The company reflects the philosophy established by the founders, based on Psalm 68:11,
"The Lord gave the word and great was the company of those who published it."

Cover design by Samson Lim
Interior design by Honeylette Pino

Published in the United States of America

ISBN: 978-1-68118-581-1
1. Self-Help / Motivational & Inspirational
2. Self-Help / Self-Management / General
15.01.29

CONTENTS

Introduction....................7
Money, Time, and Health....................9
Faith....................13
Positive Attitude....................15
Happiness Is Just a Thought Away....................17
We Can Learn from Animals....................19
Living in the Moment....................21
Fear, Knowledge, and Truth....................23
The Power of the Mind....................27
Creation's Universal Law of Attraction....................29
The Universal Computer....................33

Our Creator Has Put Us in Control 35
List of Basic Rules 37
The Blueprint 41
It's Your Choice 45
Assignments 47

INTRODUCTION

This small but powerful handbook was written to bring about a more peaceful and harmonious lifestyle for everyone. It presents a simple idea or concept that could change the way we think and live our lives. It is not new, but it has been proven over and over throughout history. I have presented it in a more simplified way for all to read and comprehend.

MONEY, TIME, AND HEALTH

Most of us have no idea what would make us truly happy, and yet we are constantly seeking it.

We all know what our basic needs are to survive: clothing on our backs, a roof over our heads, and food, not to mention love and companionship. Some people would say that they would be happy just to have all of that and to be free of worry about where the next meal was coming from. I have learned that most people believe that if they just had more money, more time, and better health, they would be happy. So how does one find more money, more time, and better health?

Most people work so hard at making a living that they don't have the time or energy to find ways to live better, healthier lives. However, we see people win the lottery or become rich and famous, but they're still unable to live happy lives. They get involved in drugs and make really bad choices in their pursuit to be happy. They overeat, drink, gamble, and engage in other habits that introduce pain and sadness into their lives.

We also see people who seem to be working hard all the time and living from paycheck to paycheck, but they are smiling, laughing, and enjoying life. We find people who are in wheelchairs and on crutches or who have other disabilities, but they are living life to the fullest. What is it that makes things different between these individuals?

I believe that it is their attitudes. No matter how much money you have or how much free time you have, these things alone will not make you happy. Even if you're in perfect health, without the right attitude you will not find happiness. Over the years, the hardest thing I have been able to find for myself or teach my children is how to be truly happy.

Happiness does not always mean the same thing for each individual. We all have different things that give us short moments of pleasure. We all have pretty much the same basic needs. Can meeting those basic needs make us truly happy?

We have seen what has happened to some people, those who were fortunate enough to have all their needs met but who still could not find true happiness. So how can we teach anyone how to be happy and how to enjoy life to the fullest?

How does one find true happiness? If you ask most people this question, they will tell you that you need faith. So let us talk about that for a moment.

FAITH

One of the key elements to finding happiness is faith. Faith is having something to believe in. Some people connect the feeling of happiness to some sinful indulgence. Some believe you must be good before good things can happen for you. Some believe that if it feels good and tastes good, it's okay to do it even if it is sinful and wrong.

Others will tell you that one must work hard and suffer to find any real reward on earth or in heaven. Can you have faith without being religious? Yes, of course, you can.

Faith is believing in something you cannot see or prove. Believing in someone is having faith in someone. Being faithful to someone is being loyal and honest with them. I believe we should also have faith in ourselves. Along with faith, we should mention hope.

Hope is looking forward with the desire and reasonable confidence that something good will happen. It is placing trust in someone and relying on that person when conditions do not warrant it. It is having expectations and believing in a centered, desirable outcome. When one has this feeling of faith and hope, all your needs and desires are going to be met. I would assume one would also have a feeling of gratitude as well as faith and hope. We should have a way to express that feeling of gratitude. So how would one express it?

Charity is the virtue that comes to mind. It is the act of giving to others without expectations of material rewards. It is the giving of your time and material resources for the benefit of others.

This is not about religion. It is about having faith in one's self and hope for a better life style, as well as having the heart and soul to give.

I mentioned that your mental attitude is the one thing that everyone has to express their feelings. Those that have a poor or negative attitude will express themselves as unhappy, angry, sick, and emotionally unstable. Those that show a positive mental attitude express themselves as happy, joyous, healthy, and emotionally stable.

POSITIVE ATTITUDE

I have found over the years that the biggest difference between those that are happy and those that are not is attitude. It's not money, wealth, or environment that makes the difference but one's own mental attitude.

Think about it. When we have a negative or pessimistic attitude, we are not the only ones that are miserable. We make everyone around us miserable.

If one is miserable, he has no chance to be happy. So we have to ask ourselves. Why would we continue to be negative? We can make choices about our lives, our jobs, and our environment. If these things are causing a negative mental attitude, change them. We need to take a good look at ourselves. Then we need to change the way we think so we can be happy.

Did you know that happiness can be just a thought away? A lot of research has gone into figuring out how we can get the most out of life and how we can find happiness. But we have come to find out that our minds can only one thought at a time.

So many people choose to worry, have pessimistic attitudes, and think the worst about others. Then they complain about what they have and don't have. But our conscious brain can only hold one thought at a time. Why do we choose to think negative thoughts that make us miserable and unhappy? Is our subconscious brain of old habits and memories controlling our conscious mind?

With just one simple change of thought, we could feel differently. We can truly find happiness just a thought away.

HAPPINESS IS JUST A THOUGHT AWAY

I believe this is true—that all we have to do is think it and we can become happy. Why can't we use this ability to create a lifestyle of joy and happiness? How do we just think and be happy? If it was easy, everyone would be doing it. My answer to this is that we can change the way we think.

We all have the ability to make our own choices and create our own lives. The real problems we face are the habits we have created for ourselves and the way we think. When we let fear and worry influence our thinking, we lose control of our thoughts and emotions. If we do not take control of our thoughts and emotions, we can and will be influenced by those around us and by our environment.

At this time, a majority of us have habits that allow us to be influenced by negative emotions. Knowledge and truth are the tools that make it possible for individuals to overcome their environment and not be influenced by it.

WE CAN LEARN FROM ANIMALS

Let's take a look at an anthill. All the ants are working hard for the winter. They gather up little bites of food and take them down into their holes in the ground. As you watch them, they are marching right along and getting out of each other's way. They are going back and forth on several little paths, and nothing seems to bother them. And then a little boy takes a stick and stirs up the anthill and scatters the ants in all directions. Then the boy sits down and watches the ants. They go right back to work, putting all the little grains of dirt back in their places and going about their business of storing food for the winter.

Have you ever noticed, for example, a chicken? It has a small brain; however, when it's under attack, it reacts and does what it needs to do to survive. It may get a few injuries, but once the attack is over, it goes back to doing what it would normally do, pecking and eating away as if nothing had happened.

It is the same on the plains of Africa. When an animal is attacked by a lion and is wounded, the animal escapes and returns to the herd. It then acts like everything is normal. Does it worry about tomorrow or what could possibly happen later in the day or next week? No, because it lives in the moment; it's enjoying eating grass now and enjoying the company of the herd. Is it thinking about its wounds, the pain, or about dying? No! Its brain is in the moment. The animal is totally there on the plains, enjoying life.

We as humans need to spend more time just living and enjoying the moment. Many people spend all their time working and thinking about the future or the past, and then they wonder why their lives are so miserable.

LIVING IN THE MOMENT

To begin to be happy, we must learn to live in the moment, to enjoy what is going on now. If you are thinking or worrying about a future event that may or may not happen, you may miss out on the pleasure of the moment. Like most people, we all spend a great deal of time just daydreaming. However, it should be a productive daydream. It should be during a relaxing time, a time that has been set aside for planning and meditating.

How do we start thinking and living in the moment? How can we work and make a living? How can we take care of our responsibilities? How can we be concerned about the future and not worry? The answer will surprise you. We can do all those things. It is simple: we plan and act without fear or worry. If you have faith and believe that all your desires are going to be granted, I believe you could easily live in the moment.

Are you focused on what you're doing at work? Lots of people just go through the motions, dragging out the day in a daze. This is not living in the moment. When you are daydreaming throughout your day, you are less productive, and you can't enjoy your work.

When you are focused on what you're doing, the time seems to pass without you noticing. Just as when you're playing, time passes by quickly, and you hate to stop what you are doing. It takes just as much energy to work as it does to play.

Why does play seem so much easier than work? The reason is that our minds are more focused on play because we are enjoying it. We should focus more on work and enjoy it or find a job that we can enjoy.

For us to overcome our fears and worries, we need faith that what we are doing is going to provide us with all our needs and desires. When we know that all our desires and needs are coming true, we can live in the moment, enjoy it, and be happy. We must overcome our fears. With knowledge and truth, we can overcome fear.

FEAR, KNOWLEDGE, AND TRUTH

Let us take a look at our natural response when someone throws a ball at us. Our hands go up to protect our face. Do we think about it before we respond? No. If we catch it, it would be because we are expecting it and are planning for it.

How about when we stumble and fall? It would not be expected; however, we react by putting our arms out with our palms down to catch ourselves. What about the times we react without thinking, like when a car pulls out in front of us? For a moment, we only feel fear. There would be no joy, anger, or pain. However, we do react, and because of previous training and experience, we slam on the brakes.

Did we think, or was it a subconscious reaction?

We can assume that it was a subconscious reaction. With the right knowledge, experience, and training, we can react subconsciously. When we train for sports (like boxing, for example), we are trained to defend ourselves without thinking. We are trained to react with different swings and blows.

Let's take a look at firemen, police officers, or the military. They are trained to react and not think in different circumstances. During my own training in the navy, we would train and train so that our reaction would be one of habit and not of thought.

Most emergency situations require you to react without thinking. So if the mind can be trained to react subconsciously, then we should be able to train our thoughts to be positive. We could and should develop a habit of positive thinking. You can learn to react in a positive, productive way subconsciously.

So one of the things we need is knowledge and the truth. There have been lots of books written on positive thinking. There are also books about living in the moment. We can find books on meditation, yoga, spiritual thinking, and prayer. All these books can teach us to bring happiness and joy into our lives.

We can also learn about karma and the laws of attraction. Karma is a Buddhist belief that teaches that if we do good, we will be rewarded. The laws of attraction believe that by doing good, you will also attract good things into your life. However, it also teaches that we must believe it will happen, that we must have faith and gratitude and keep a positive attitude for the law to work.

I believe it is more than just a law of attraction. Have you ever started laughing? After a moment, people around you will begin to join in your laughter. Just smile at people, and they will smile back.

Think about this. We can actually pass on happiness to other people just from a smile. When we keep a positive attitude, this law of attraction does work. Kindness rewards kindness, and anger creates more anger. Our minds are more powerful than the average person can realize.

THE POWER OF THE MIND

Have you ever read or heard the story of the 120-pound mother who lifted a car off her child? How about the person who cut off his own arm while he was alone in the desert and was hanging from a cliff to survive? Did you hear of the cancer patient who remained calm and who, because of her faith in God, was healed by prayer?

How about the story of the man who survived a plane crash? He was paralyzed, had numerous injuries, and was unable to speak. He could only communicate by blinking his eyes. The doctors told him that he would never walk or move. They told him that he would be a vegetable, that he would need assistance to breathe, and that he would be on life support for the rest of his life. His mind refused to accept it. And with just his mind and a positive attitude, he changed his life.

He was determined to not only survive but also to walk out of that hospital. And with a positive mind, he forced himself to strengthen his lungs. He slowly worked on all parts of his body with his mind. It was only nine months later that with some help, he was able to walk out of the hospital. He also regained his speech. He now goes around the country giving lectures on the power of positive thinking. The idea that a positive mental attitude can change your life is real. By just knowing it, you can begin to change your life.

There have been stories of prisoners of war who survived captivity and torture because they used their minds. With faith and attitude, they were able to live through the ordeal.

There was also this patient who kept going back to the doctor for these terrible headaches. The doctor examined the patient and could find no reason or cause for her pain. He gave her the mental attitude of faith and convinced her that he had the only medication that could possibly help her. The pill was just a sugar pill, and the patient was cured of her migraines. She was mentally able to heal herself because she believed in the medication.

Your mind can be a great engine that can take you where you want to go, but you must also take action.

CREATION'S UNIVERSAL LAW OF ATTRACTION

Most people will try to do the right thing in life to make themselves happy and prosperous. They work hard and go to church. They try to do what their parents had taught them. But they still struggle to find happiness. They fall short because they lose faith and give up when things don't happen right away. They get discouraged or change their minds, and they go off in a different direction.

You may have heard that if you focus on one thing, the universe will bring it to you. One of the things you must have is faith—faith in yourself, faith in the universe, and faith in what you have learned and what you're about to learn.

Lots of successful people will tell you that if you focus and believe in something hard and long enough, the opportunity will come to you. They had faith in themselves. When given the right amount of time, the universe will create your desired wishes.

Have you ever noticed that some things seem to work out right despite themselves? God took six days to create the heavens and the earth. Just think how long it's going to take for the universe to conceive and carry out all our wishes and goals.

I believe the Creator wants us all to be happy, healthy, and wealthy. I believe he gave us all the power to create for ourselves through our choices. The problem is, we make very bad choices and thus create hell on earth. You must give the universe the time it needs to create the right environment to achieve your desired goals.

God wants to please us and give us all our wants and needs. The problem with most people is that they put in so many requests at once and have no real, solid goals. When your mind is jumping from one thought to another, the universe is working hard just to satisfy one thing, only to be bombarded with another. And when you add in poor attitudes and hateful and bad behaviors, it has to abort mission after mission because of our own bad choices. And then you wonder, *Why is my life so mixed up?*

When you have faith, you must also have hope. Hope is the feeling of joy in knowing that your desires will be granted.

THE UNIVERSAL COMPUTER

This may sound strange at first, but what if the universe is acting like one big computer? The only language this computer understands is thoughts. God has programmed the computer to react without emotions, right or wrong. No matter how good or how bad you are, the computer is trying to grant you your wishes based on your thoughts.

You say, "I want to be rich," but your mind is thinking, *It's not going to happen.* The universal computer is programmed and is acting only on your thoughts and not your wishes. You keep thinking, *It is not going to happen.* So the universe is going to act on your mental command. It does not happen.

"Be careful what you wish for." I'm sure you have heard this before. You are what you think, and you attract what you think. Your mind can attract unwanted actions in your life. The thought *I'm never going to be happy* is like a command to the universal law of attraction to not make you happy. *I'm too fat.* The law responds. You think you're fat, so you remain fat. *I'm feeling sick.* The law responds. You become sick. *I'm so poor.* The law responds. You become poor.

What if you are what you feel? What if the universe can also respond to feelings and not just thoughts? What if it only understands and reacts to feelings and thoughts?

You go to a party, and in one corner, everyone is happy, smiling, and having fun. And then on the other side of the room, everyone is sad and quiet. If you listen in on each side, you will find that the happy side is feeling joyous because someone there is very happy. You listen in on the quiet side and find that someone is sad or even angry. So everyone starts to feel those same emotions.

God's most precious gift to us is the ability to make a choice. Most people will say they cannot control themselves. Really? The truth is, we have created mental habits that just seem uncontrollable. God gave us the power to choose not just between good or bad. We have the power to choose how to learn and think and reason.

OUR CREATOR HAS PUT US IN CONTROL

The very way we think and solve problems has become a learned habit. Once we realize this, we can control our minds and change that habit. We can actually create a habit of a positive attitude. With this attitude, we can create a much more harmonious and happy environment for us all.

Now that we know the truth about ourselves and our environment, we can actually make mental choices to change our lives. We can train ourselves to have faith and hope. We can create a habit of doing good. We can create a habit of taking care of our bodies and making them healthier.

So what must we do to get started on following this lifestyle of faith, hope, and charity? I also say charity because once you begin to have this most wonderful feeling of a positive mental attitude, you will see that it also comes from your charity. We must also have some rules to follow to avoid those bad choices. We must have a plan to go by before we start to draw up the blueprints to healthy, wealthy, and happy lifestyles.

LIST OF BASIC RULES

1. Show gratitude for what we have. We must thank our Creator for all that we have and all that we will receive. We must first accept all our blessings and show gratitude to all those around us. Once we are grateful for all that we have, we can learn to love ourselves and life. With gratitude comes charity.
2. Follow the Golden Rule: we must always treat everyone the way we want to be treated. We must learn to do this without exception and without any expectations. We do this to make others and ourselves feel good. We leave the choice up to others on how they will feel and respond.
3. Pride has no room in your blueprint. A negative pride is full of arrogance, conceit, and a feeling of superiority. It is the first among the seven deadly sins. As a virtue,

it's equivalent to personal dignity, worth, honor, and self-respect, but it can also make us proud. We must be humble and modest and forget our foolish pride.

4. Take responsibility for your life. Realize that your own choices got you where you are today, and it will be your choices that will carry you through to the rest of your life.
5. Your subconscious mind cannot distinguish between what is real and what is imaginary. So when you find yourself worrying and thinking negative thoughts, make the choice to overcome that negative thinking. Know that it's an imaginary thought. Command yourself to stop. Instead, focus on your goals and how great you feel. Let your mind and body feel as if all your wishes have been fulfilled.
6. Always pay it forward. Believe that all that is given joyfully will be returned tenfold. When you help others, you help yourself. Charity is a form of gratitude for all that you have and all that you will receive. Feel it in your heart and soul.
7. Accept the blessings of others when they are offered. Accept help from others when it is needed. Be grateful for the smallest acts of kindness, even a small compliment. Be grateful and accept it with joy, for in doing so, you also bless them. Their act of kindness is making them feel good, and by accepting it, you also make them feel good.

8. Help others in humble silence, and you bless yourself. It will give you a deeper satisfaction for your own self-worth. You have the power to create a better life for yourself and others.

THE BLUEPRINT

Now that you have rules to follow, you must now create a plan of action. Create a blueprint for creating a healthy, wealthy, and happy lifestyle. You must study and plan daily. This is your drawing, your plan, your blueprint.

You must decide what it is that would really make you happy. Put it down on paper. List your desires and wants on paper or in a journal. Put your most desirable wants on a corkboard with pictures and bold letters. Place it in a picture frame or tape it to a mirror or a desktop. Put it somewhere you can see and admire it daily. Review and adjust them as you progress.

Every morning, thank your Creator for all that you have and be thankful for all that you are going to receive. Remind yourself all throughout the day to be grateful. The feeling of gratitude is humbling. Write down all your blessings. Put them on paper where you can see them and love your life.

Let your gratitude be the last thing on your mind at night. Thank your Creator for all that you have and all that is going to be given to you. Let your subconscious mind believe that you have already gotten them and imagine how you're going to feel. Let yourself feel as if it has already happened.

Be happy! Live your life as you have always dreamed it would be. You must stay positive and focused on today. Enjoy today for all your wants and needs have been put in place. Have faith in the universe. Let the universe go to work. Know that it's all going to come your way somehow. Know that as long as you have hope and maintain a positive attitude, you will be happy. Know that nothing will change the final outcome of your request.

All your desires will be given to you with the right opportunity and patience. When the universe shows you an opportunity, you will be able to make the right choice to take advantage of it. When you desire a better job, it is going to come your way. When you desire more money, the opportunity for more money will be given to you. When you desire better health, you will see and do what it takes to improve your health. Have faith that you will by choice see the opportunities and take them.

The universe is yours, and it is programmed to give you the opportunity to make choices. By choice you can make all your desires possible.

Do not be distracted from your desires or from a positive mental attitude. Create a habit of thinking positively. Be determined to create a happy and joyous lifestyle. Reinforce your positive thinking with reminders. Notes and pictures create positive sayings. When asked, "How are things going?" make a habit of saying something positive back, like "I'm doing great," "Life is good," or "I'm having a great day."

Review the rules and learn to live them daily. As you follow the rules, you will begin to feel good about yourself and see all the good in those around you. Review your desires daily and adjust them as you fulfill them.

Study, plan, and learn to improve on them. Get inspirational books and pictures with quotes. Find out what makes you happy, list them down, and do what you can to achieve them. Life is truly a precious gift. Make your choices and have fun with it.

Be happy! Don't worry! Remember that it is your choice and that it's only a thought away. Life can be awesome for everyone.

IT'S YOUR CHOICE

I have written a list of assignments to help those that want to achieve a positive mental attitude create healthy, wealthy, and happy lifestyles for themselves. We have the knowledge now. We know that our attitude affects our emotions and that our emotions can attract negative or positive energy. We know that we must create a positive mental attitude. We need to form a habit of positive thinking.

These assignments are designed to help us find faith in ourselves and give us hope for better and happier lives. It will also help us achieve a habit of gratitude through charity. I have given the reader several assignments to help them focus on their own wants and needs and to give them the tools they need to create a better environment for themselves and others.

We know how powerful the mind can be just from positive thinking. Not only can it heal our bodies but it can also attract positive things into our lives.

ASSIGNMENTS

ASSIGNMENT 1

For our first assignment we should refer to our first basic rule: "Show gratitude for what we have." Make a list of all our blessings.

Let's begin with listing three blessings that have to do with our health.

1. ____________________

2. ____________________

3. ____________________

Let's list three blessings that have to do with possessions.

1. ______________________________

2. ______________________________

3. ______________________________

Let's now list three blessings that have to do with happiness

1. ______________________________

2. ______________________________

3. ______________________________

List three persons whom you are most thankful for having in your life and who help improve your health, your wealth, and your happiness.

1. ______________________________

This person helped me with health by ______________

2. ______________________________

This person helped me financially by ______________

3. ______________________________

This person helped me emotionally by ______________

What I would like for you to do now is begin to thank your Creator. Thank him for these blessings first thing every morning and every evening before you lie down to rest. Write a thank-you card to each of the individuals that you have put down as a blessing in your life. A small note or card will do. You can choose to mail it or not, but you must physically go through the motions of writing to them.

ASSIGNMENT 2

I would like for you now to list any individuals that you feel you have done wrong to or hurt in some way.

1. ______________________________
2. ______________________________
3. ______________________________

Write a letter to each telling them how sorry you are for what you have done to them and ask them to forgive you. This is for you. Once you have completed the letters, do what you want with them.

Now list any individuals that have hurt you or done you wrong.

1. ______________________________
2. ______________________________
3. ______________________________

Write each one a note forgiving them for what they have done. Once you have completed the letters, do what you want with them also. This exercise is preparing your subconscious mind for a positive mental attitude. It will help to release any negative energy left inside your subconscious mind. The negative energy hidden within us can cause emotional and physical disorder in our lives.

ASSIGNMENT 3

Now we can get down to the really fun part. In this assignment, I would like for you to list your deepest desires.

List three things concerning health, wealth, and happiness.

1. I want ____________________ concerning my health.
2. I want ____________________ to improve my wealth.
3. I want ________________________ to make me happy.

You have put your desires on paper. Your desires, goals, and wishes are now given to the universal computer. It will be up to it to find and give you the opportunity to achieve them.

ASSIGNMENT 4

What you must do now is create images of your desires. You want to feel younger and healthier. If you desire more money, a house, a job, a business, or whatever material thing you want, get pictures that will remind you of what your desires are. Place them where you can easily see them so you can be constantly reminded of them. Find things that make you feel happy. It can be music, pictures, or anything that will help you obtain the happiness you desire.

List a statement to describe the health you desire. For example: I look so young and healthy.

Then make it a thank you statement. For example: Thank you for making me so young and healthy.

1. I ______________________________

2. Thank you for ______________________________

List a statement to describe your financial desire. For example: "I want a thousand dollars."

Then make it a thank-you statement. For example: "Thank you for giving me a thousand dollars."

1. I ______________________________

2. Thank you for ______________________________

List a statement of happiness. For example: I feel great.

Then make it a statement of thanks. For example: Thank you for making me feel great.

1. I ______________________________

2. Thank you for ______________________________

ASSIGNMENT 5

Now list three statements of a positive response to "How is your day?" or "How are you doing?" For example: "I'm doing great!" or "It's really a great day."

1. ______________________________
2. ______________________________
3. ______________________________

Practice saying one of these statements every time you need to respond. Before you continue a conversation, create a habit of positive response. Once you have created this habit, you will notice a great deal of difference in the way you feel physically. Your emotions will begin to change along with your health. You will begin to feel extremely happier.

There will be times when old habits will creep back in, human nature tells us that. So to combat old habits, we must create new and better habits. However, we need to know what those habits are. Even worry and negative thinking can be habits that need to be overcome.

ASSIGNMENT 6

In this assignment, we must identify our bad habits and create new ones to combat the bad ones.

List three things you do or don't do to cause your own bad health. For example: "I eat too much" or "I don't exercise."

1. ______________________________
2. ______________________________
3. ______________________________

List three things to combat the problems. For example: "I will eat out of a smaller bowl or eat smaller portions" or "I will walk for two hours every day at this time."

1. ______________________________
2. ______________________________
3. ______________________________

List three things that interfere with you creating wealth. For example: "I spend too much on eating out and buying junk food" or "I use the ATM too much."

1. ______________________________
2. ______________________________
3. ______________________________

List three solutions to the problem. For example: "I will limit my eating out and buying junk food" or "I will quit using ATMs."

1. ______________________________
2. ______________________________
3. ______________________________

Whatever bad habits bring about unhappiness in your life—drugs, drinking, lying, or whatever bad habits you have created—know that one of the basic rules is to realize that your choices got you where you are today and that it will be your choices that will carry you through to the rest of your life.

Here is where you will take responsibility for your life. By choice you can overcome these habits. You can and will create a better life for yourself with positive thinking.

List three things that you do that you're unhappy about. For example: "I sleep in late too much."

1. ______________________________
2. ______________________________
3. ______________________________

List your solutions to the problems. For example: "I will set my alarm and get up earlier" or "I will go to bed earlier."

1. ______________________________
2. ______________________________
3. ______________________________

Realize that habits and even the way we think are learned subconscious actions that can be overcome with a positive mental attitude. You must have a deep desire to change. The universe is programmed to give you all the opportunity to make your desires and wishes come true. It's up to you to make the choice to achieve them.

ASSIGNMENT 7

We have to overcome this habit of worry. It's human nature to be concerned about the future. So let's face them.

List three concerns about your health. For example: "I have high blood pressure."

1. ______________________________
2. ______________________________
3. ______________________________

List three ways to deal with the worry. For example: "I will consult my doctor."

1. ______________________________
2. ______________________________
3. ______________________________

List three things that concern your income. For example: "I fear I will lose my job" or "I worry about not having enough."

1. ______________________________
2. ______________________________
3. ______________________________

List three things to overcome the fear. For example: "I will get a new job" or "I will save for emergencies."

1. ____________________
2. ____________________
3. ____________________

List the one thing that you feel is keeping you from being happy. For example: "My job."

1. ____________________

List one thing to solve the problem. For example: "Change jobs."

1. ____________________

I only listed one thing that could possibly make you unhappy. Happiness means different things to each individual. This is your blueprint to finding happiness. What we already know is that a positive mental attitude can bring about change in our lives. We can find happiness.

ASSIGNMENT 8

List at least seven things that you would like to do and that could make you feel happy.

1. ____________________
2. ____________________

3. ____
4. ____
5. ____
6. ____
7. ____

Now that you have an idea of what you want to do, it's time to plan when to do all those things. Let's write in a time period to accomplish each of them.

1. Date: ___________________________________
2. Date: ___________________________________
3. Date: ___________________________________
4. Date: ___________________________________
5. Date: ___________________________________
6. Date: ___________________________________
7. Date: ___________________________________

Now that you have listed all your desires and wants on paper and you have a timetable to achieve them, set aside some time each day to meditate and think about them. Give yourself room for adjustments and then give the universal computer some time to provide you with the opportunities to achieve those desires.

It's your choice!

Thank you for allowing me to become a part of your life by taking the time to read my book. I hope you have enjoyed it. May the information and advice I have given you bring you a much happier, healthier, and prosperous life forever!

CPSIA information can be obtained at www.ICGtesting.com
Printed in the USA
LVOW10s2031080716

495161LV00004BA/5/P